My Book of Green

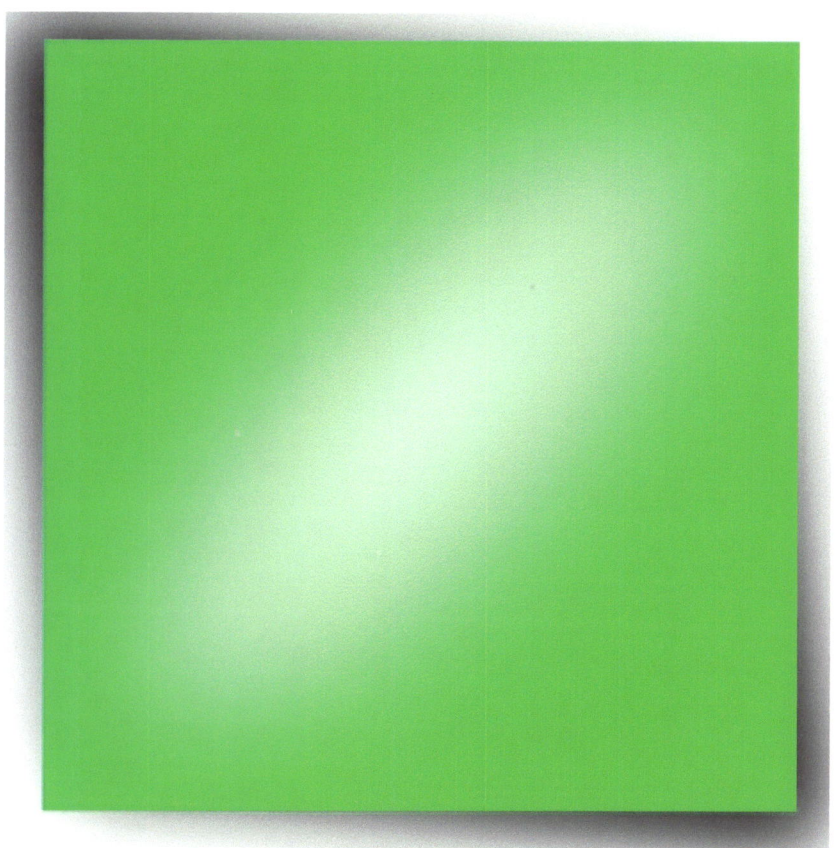

Written By: Melissa L. Bryant

I dedicate this book to my children Lavicia, Vyshonn, Damarius, Darrell and Rashad who I love so much. I dedicate this book to my grandchildren. I dedicate this book to my nieces Kyrenne and Claudia. I dedicate this book to my nephews Jarvis, Conner and Amarie. I dedicate this book to all the children at Daleville Christian Fellowship. I dedicate this book to all the children around the world. This book teaches you different things that are Green. Green is an amazing color that God has created. God bless you and the best is yet to come.

Author Melissa L. Bryant

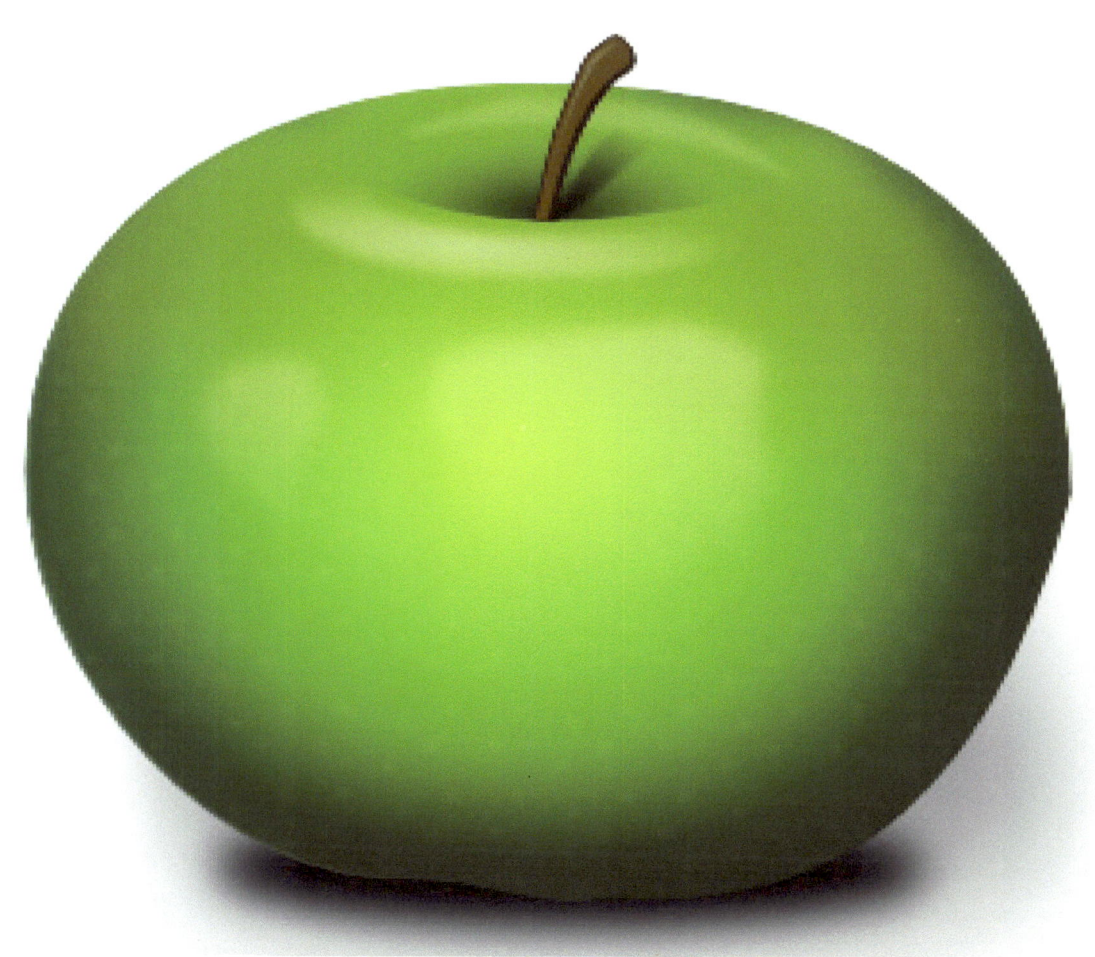

This is a green apple.

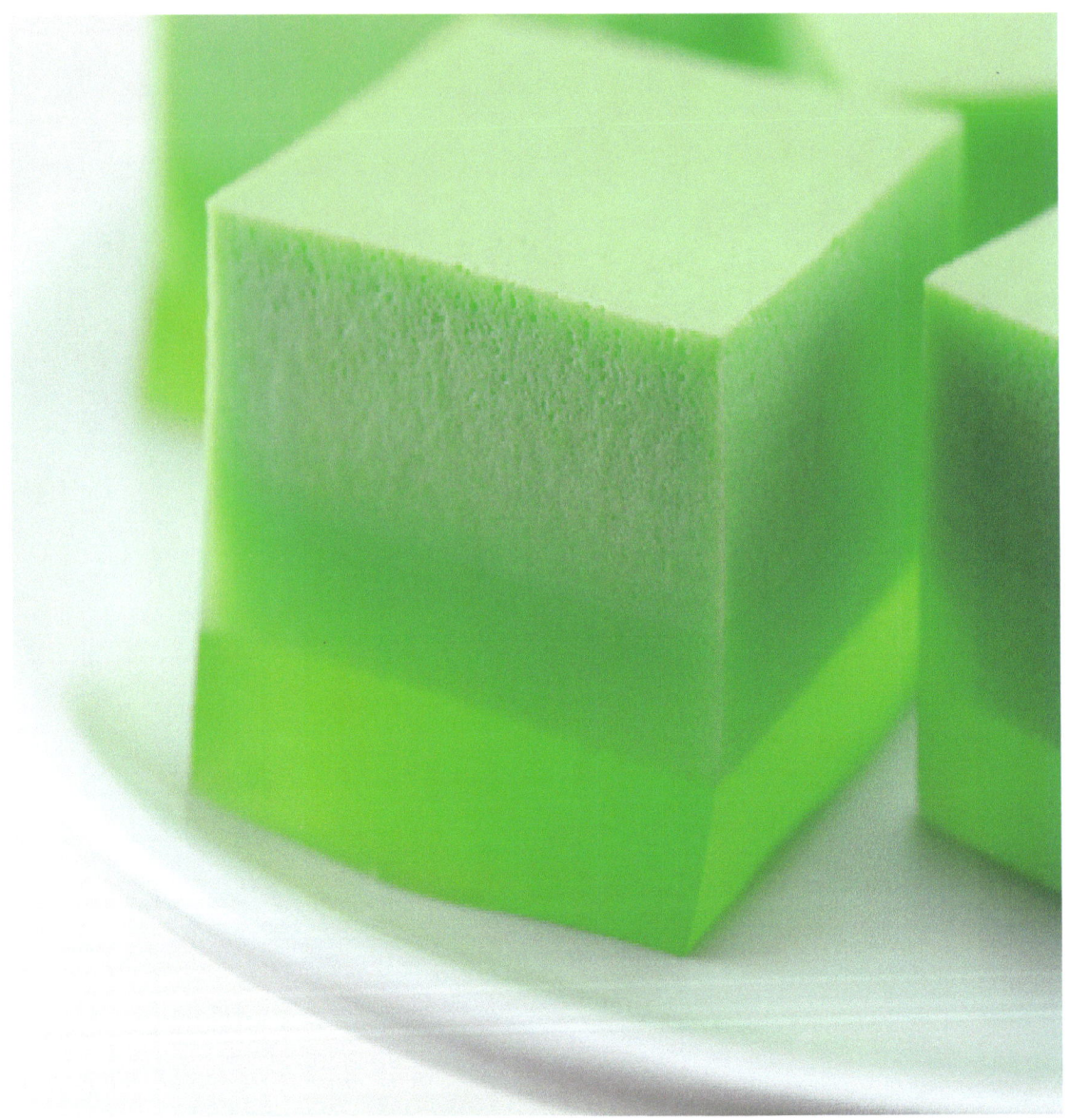

Ice cream jelly is the color green.

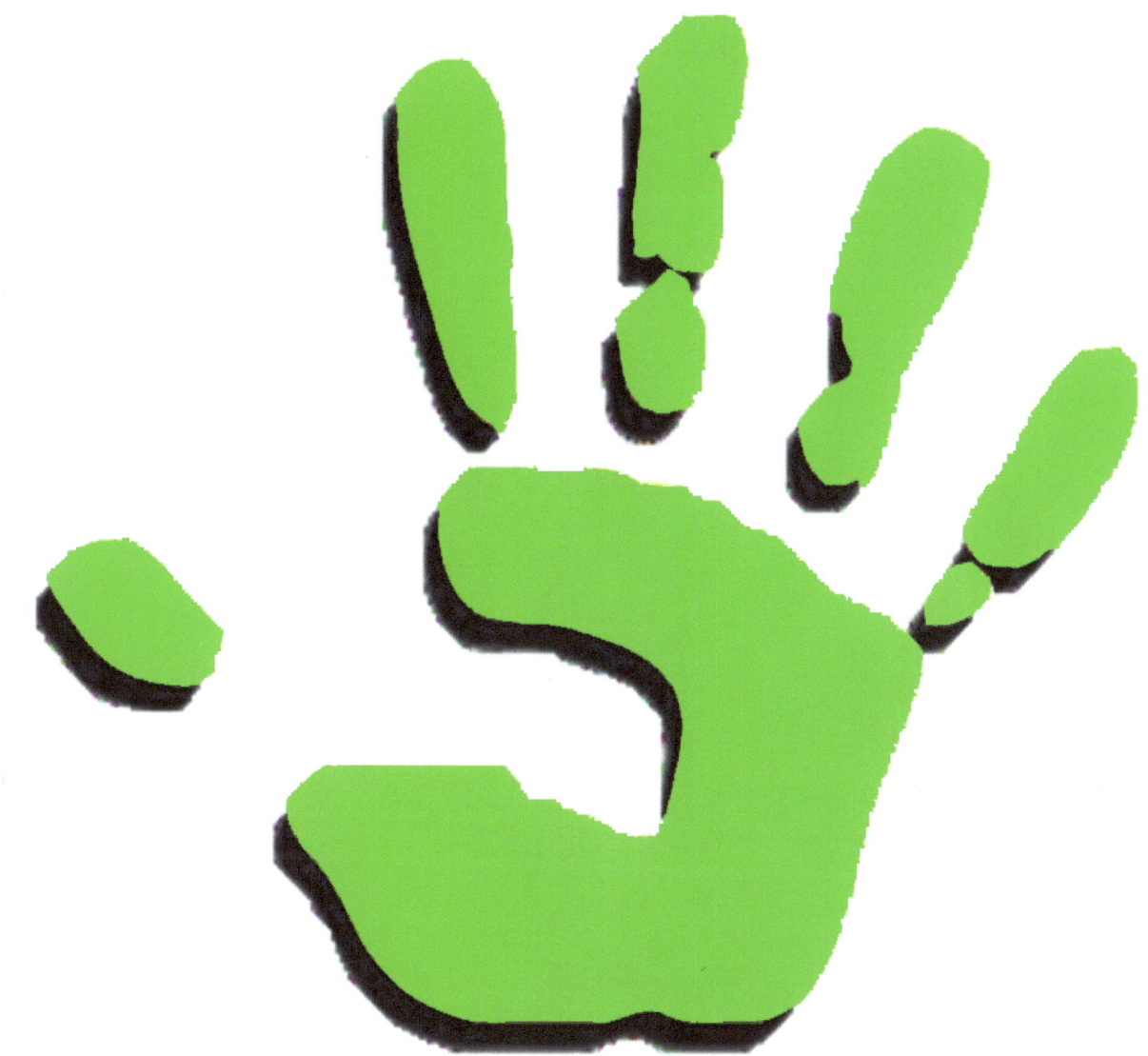

My hand is the color green.

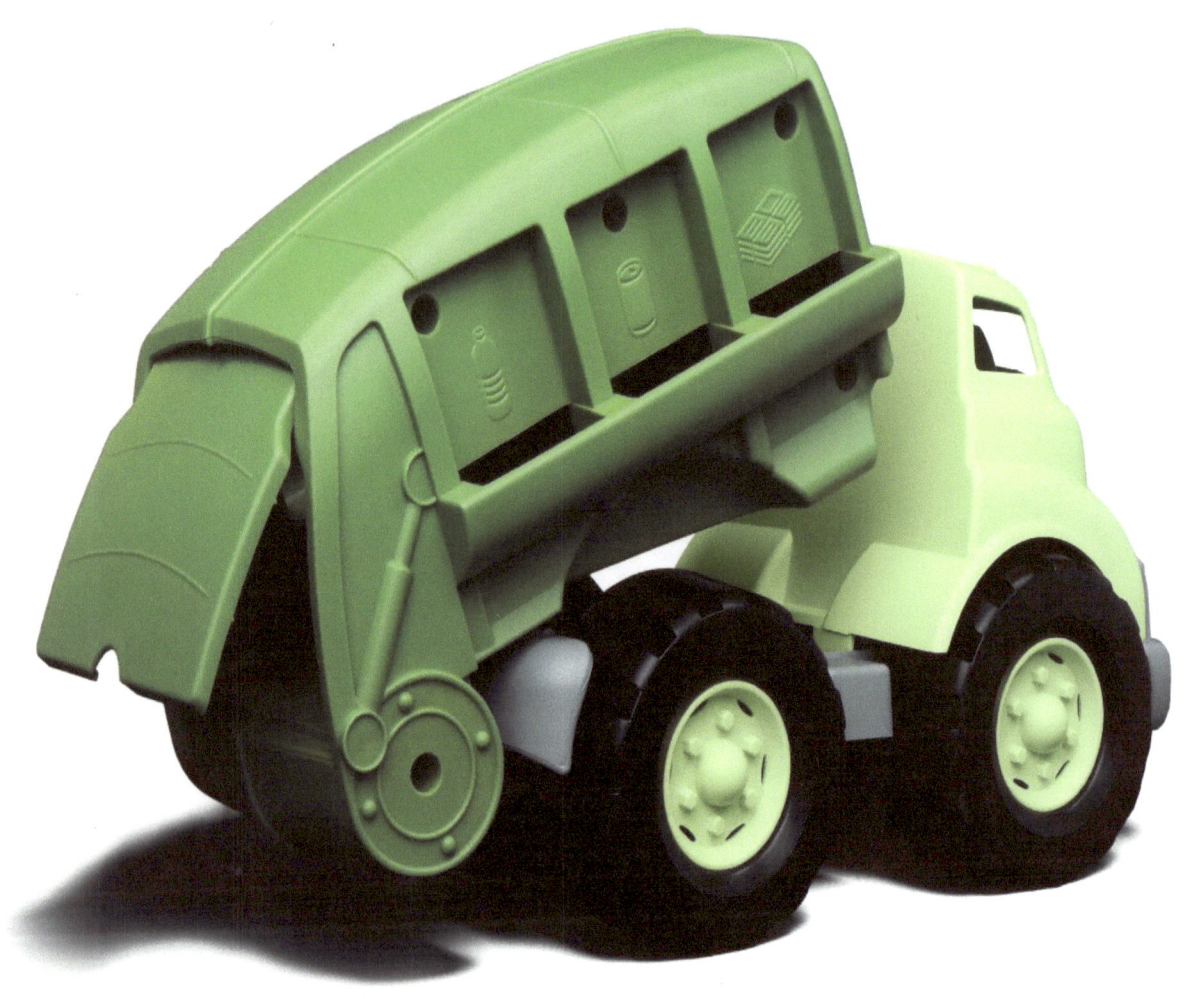

This toy truck is the color green.

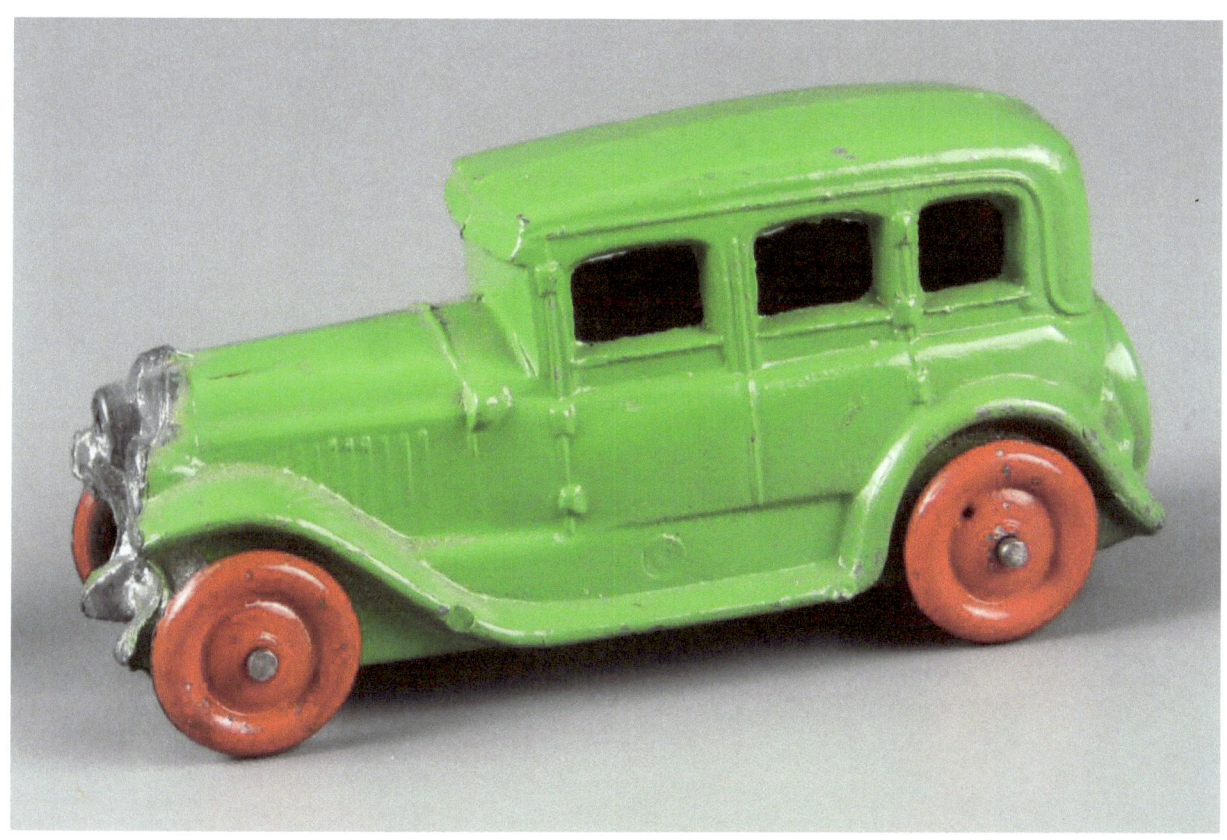

This toy car is the color green.

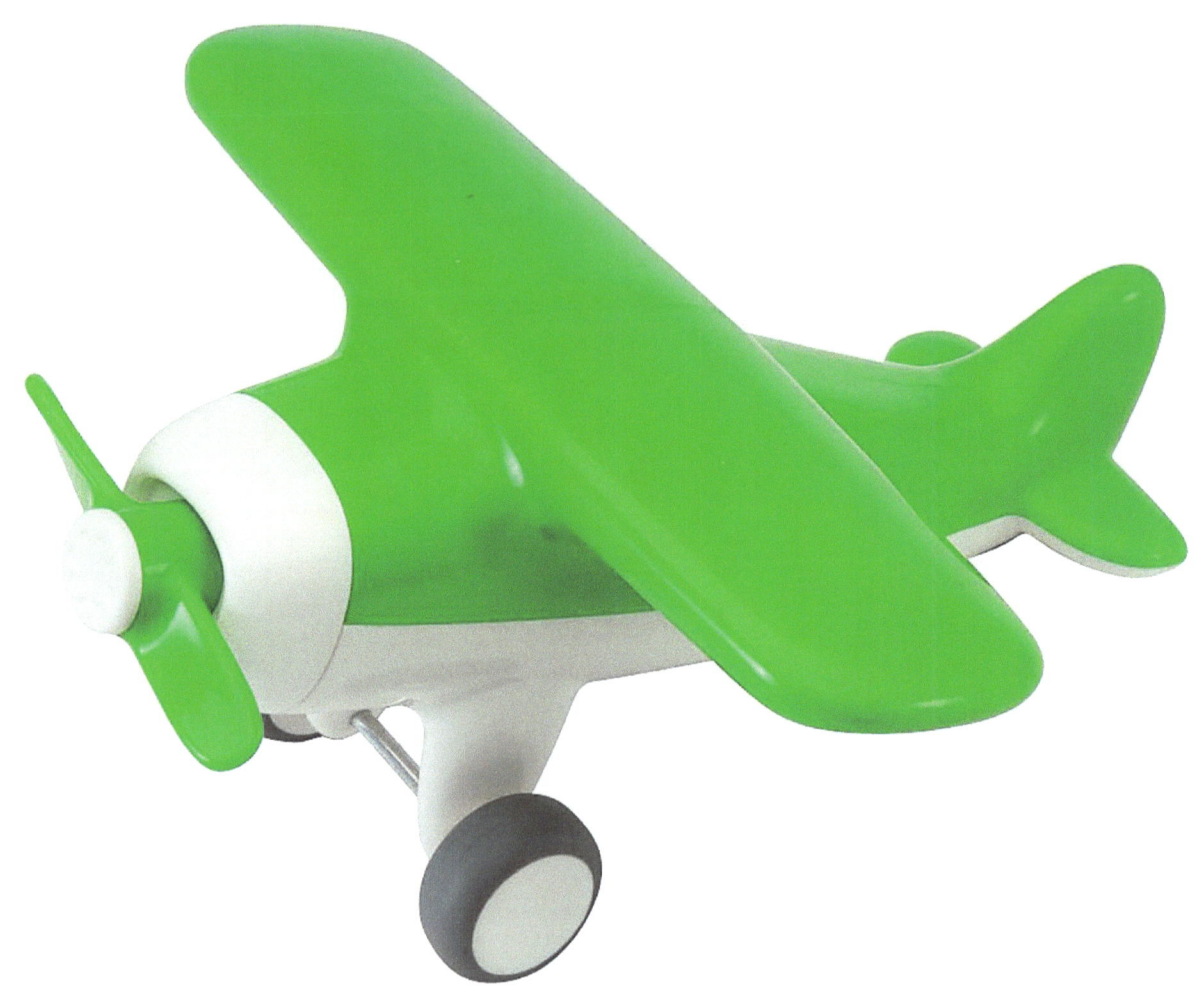

This toy airplane is the color green.

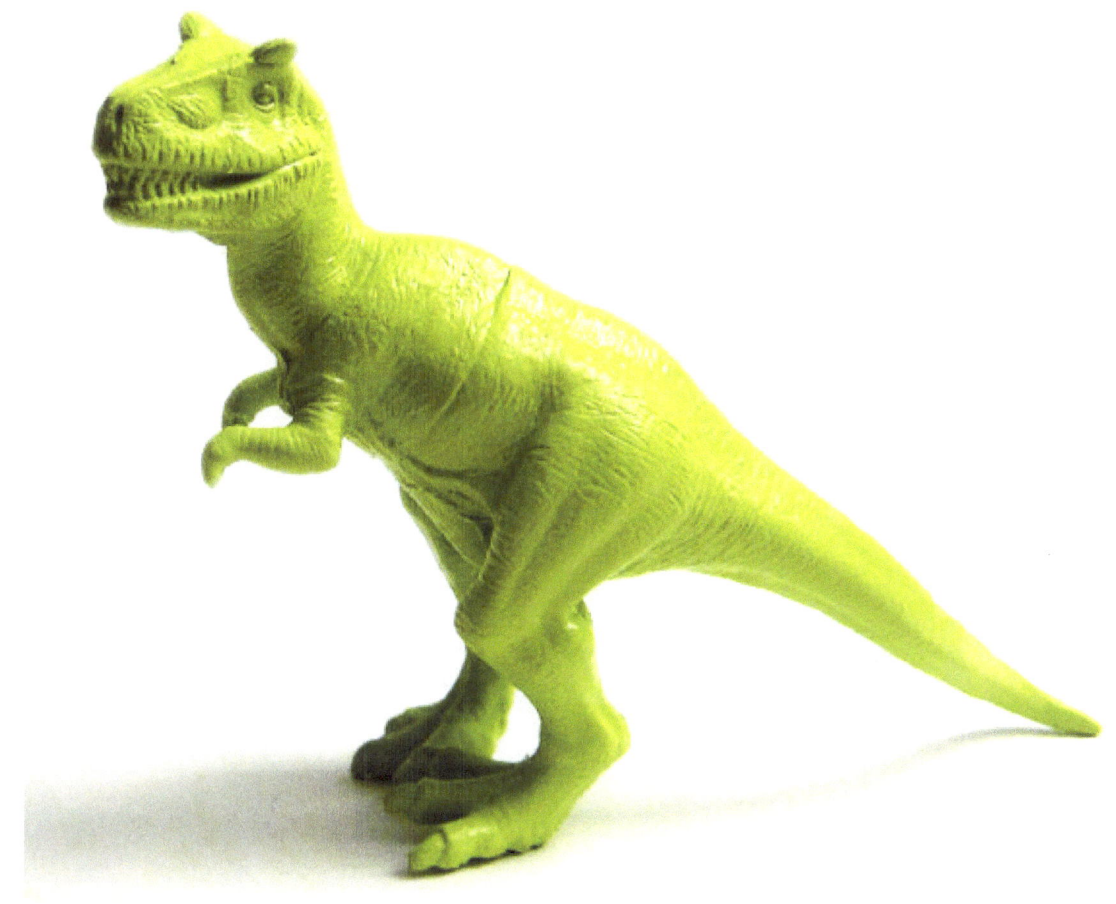

This toy dinosaur is the color green.

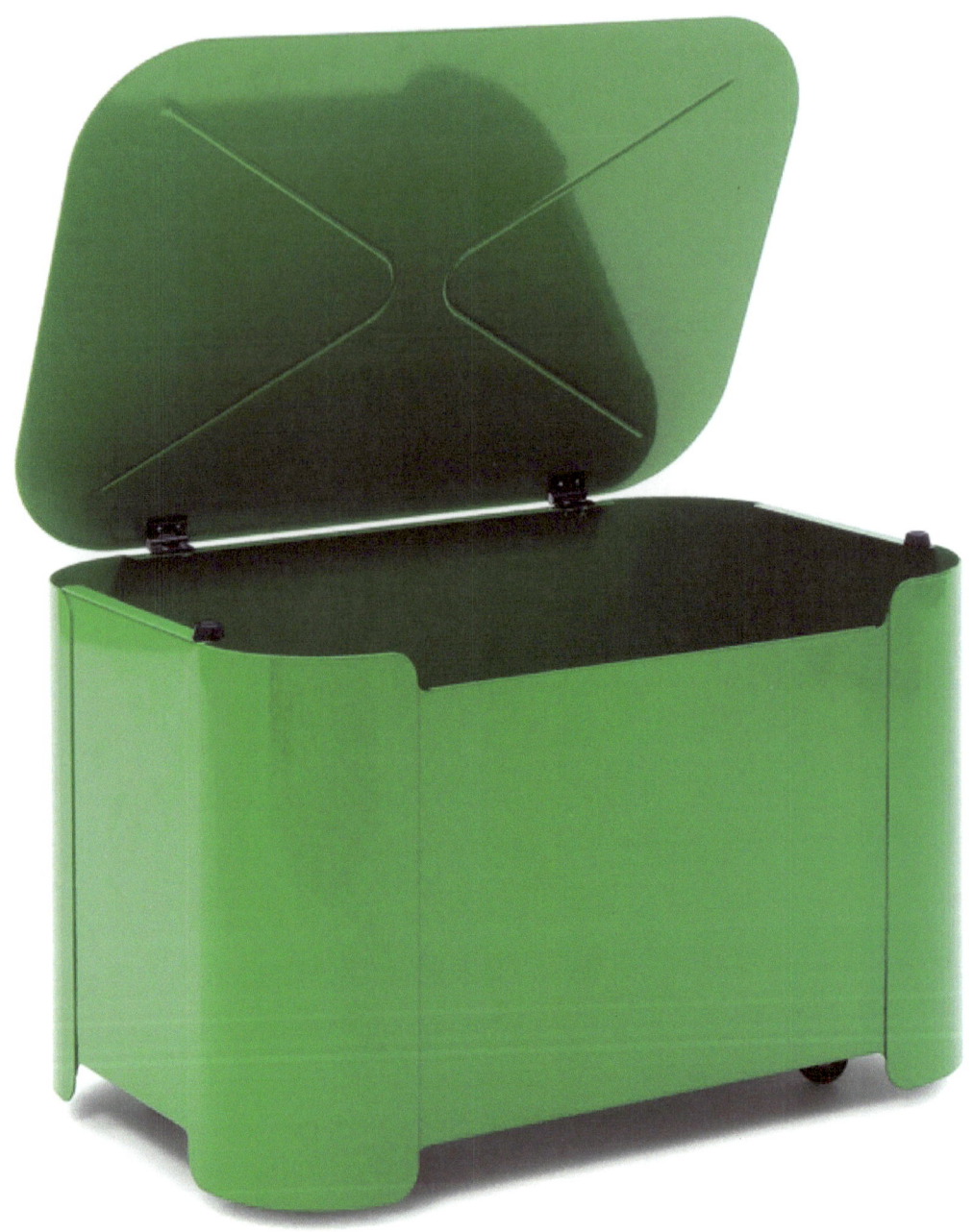

This is a green toy box.

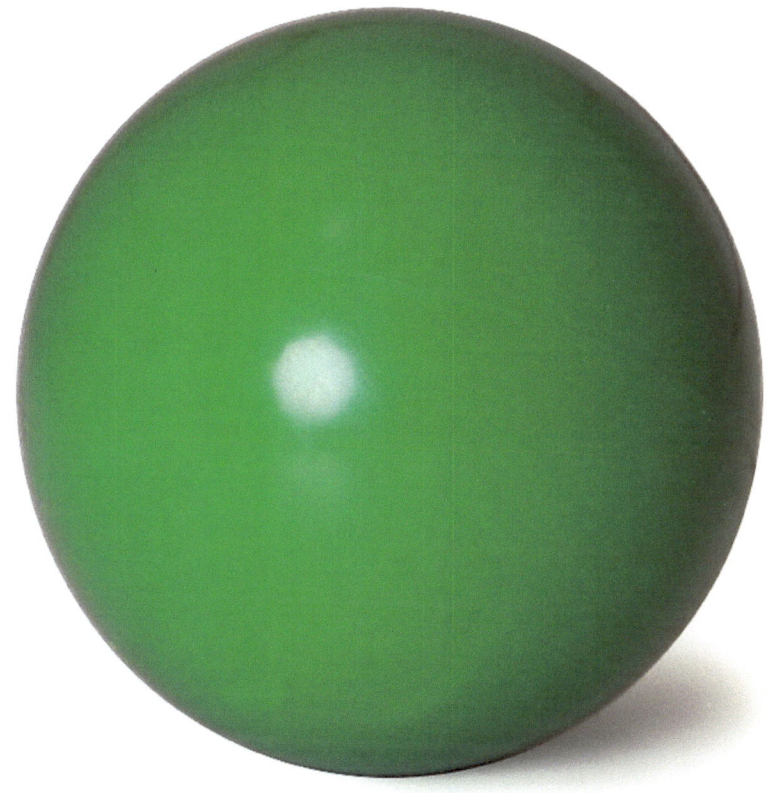

This ball is the color green.

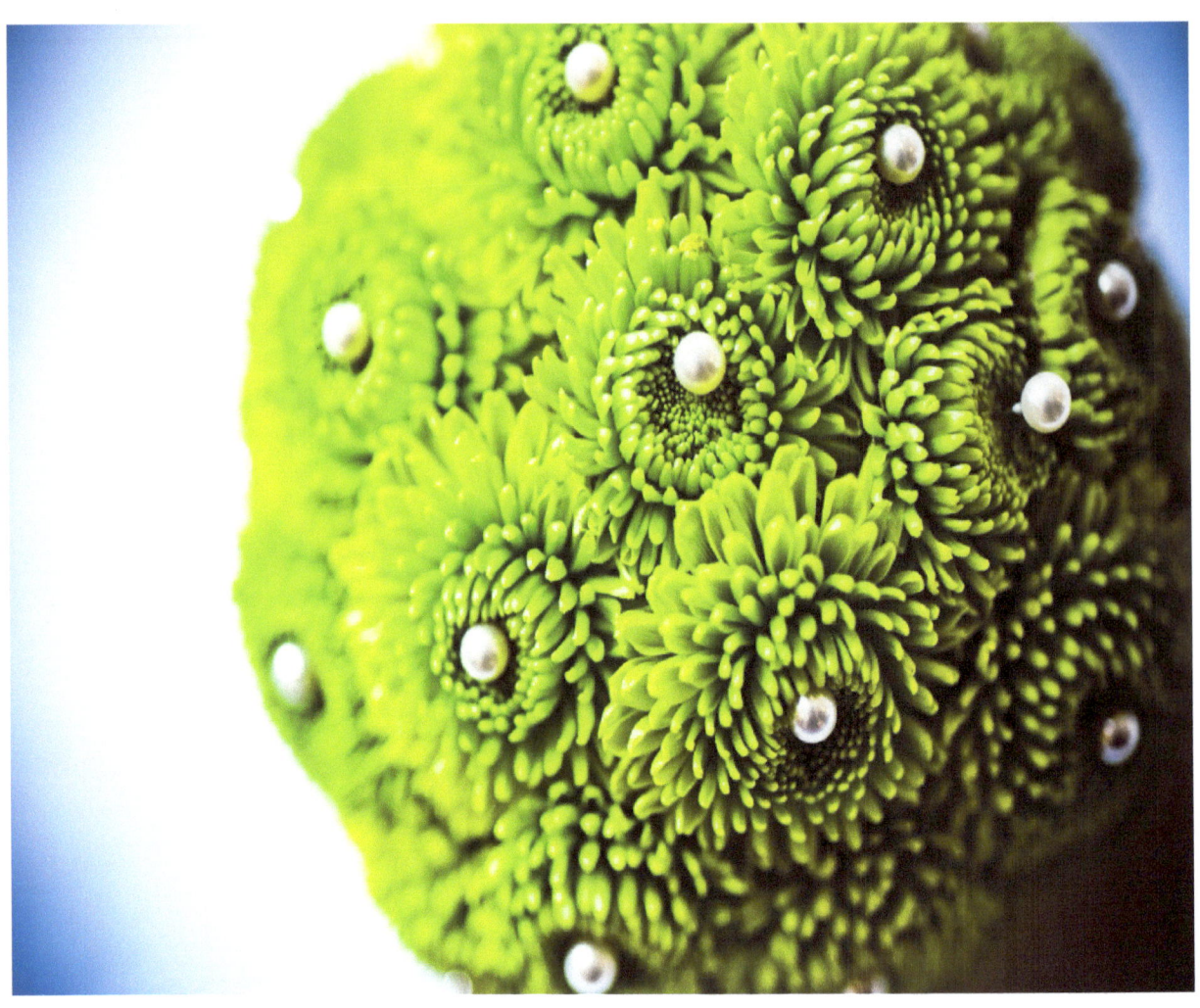

This flower is the color green.

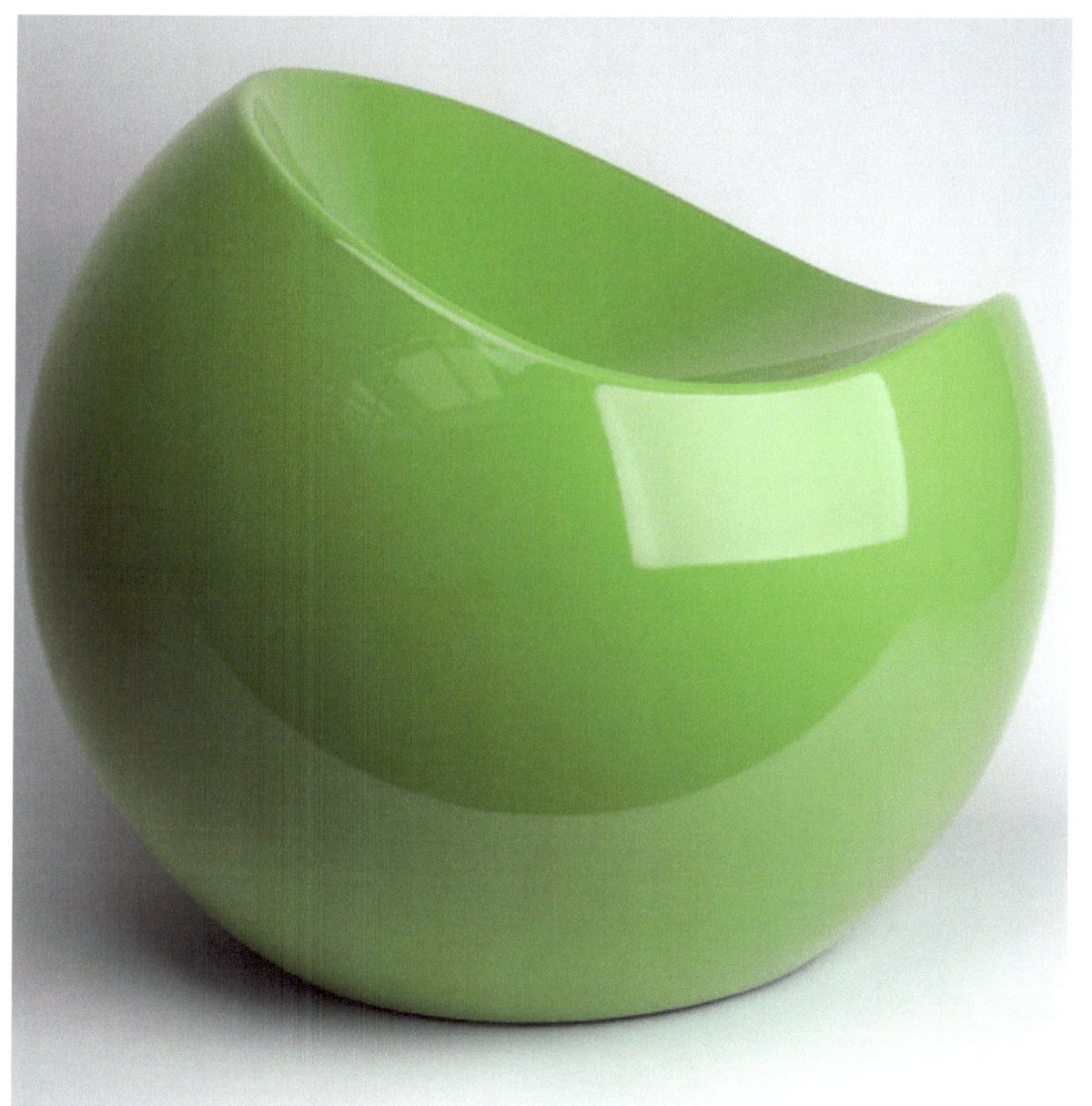

This is a green Bowling chair.

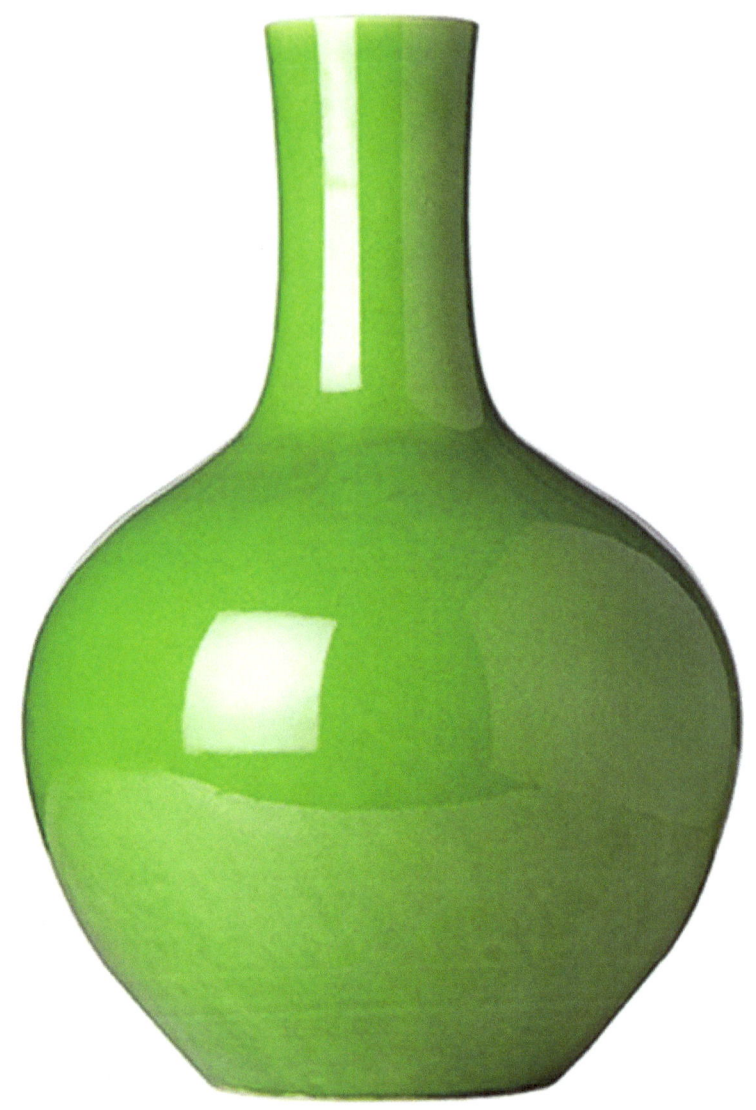

This vase is the color green.

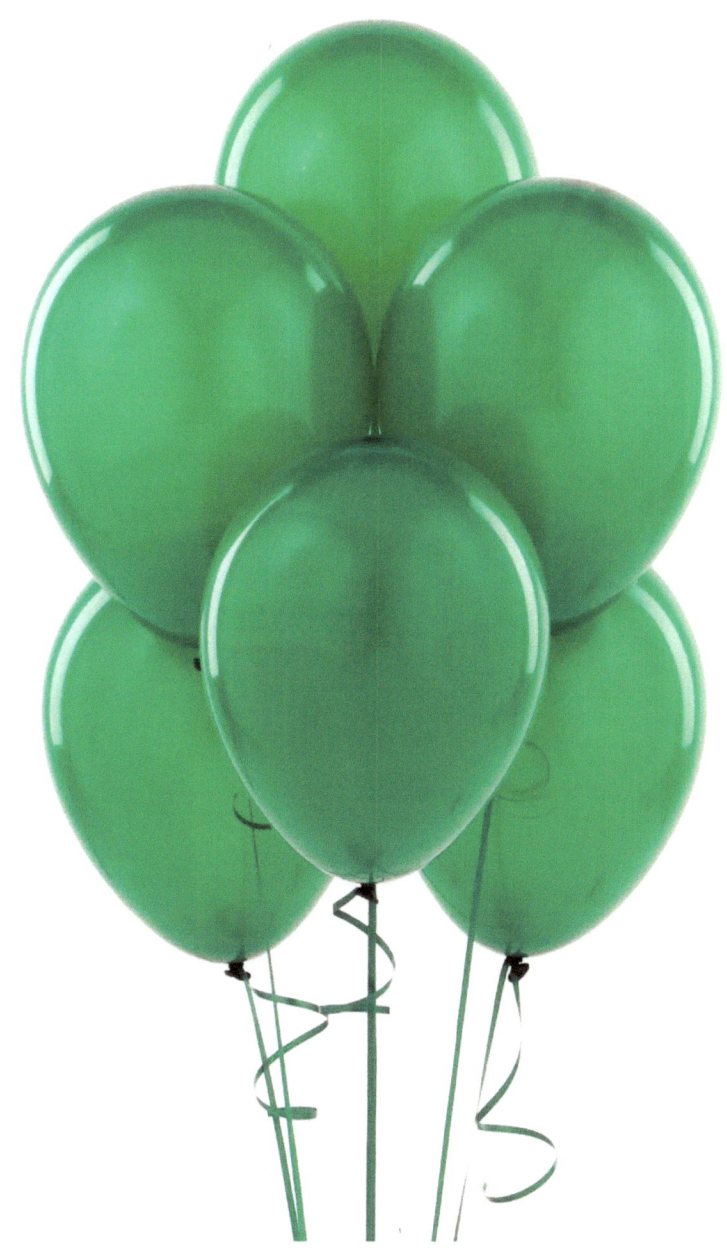

These balloons are the color green.

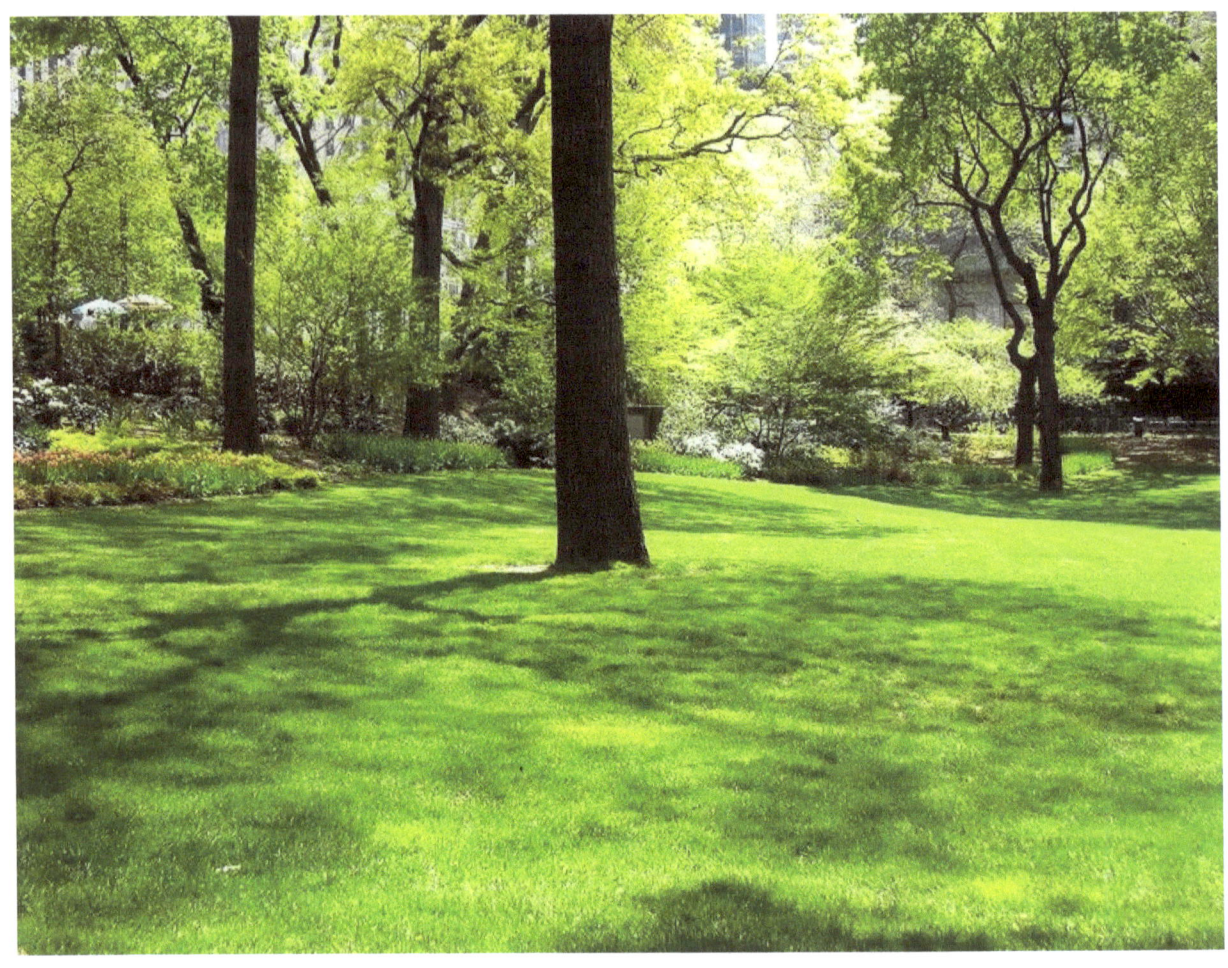

The trees and grass is the color green.

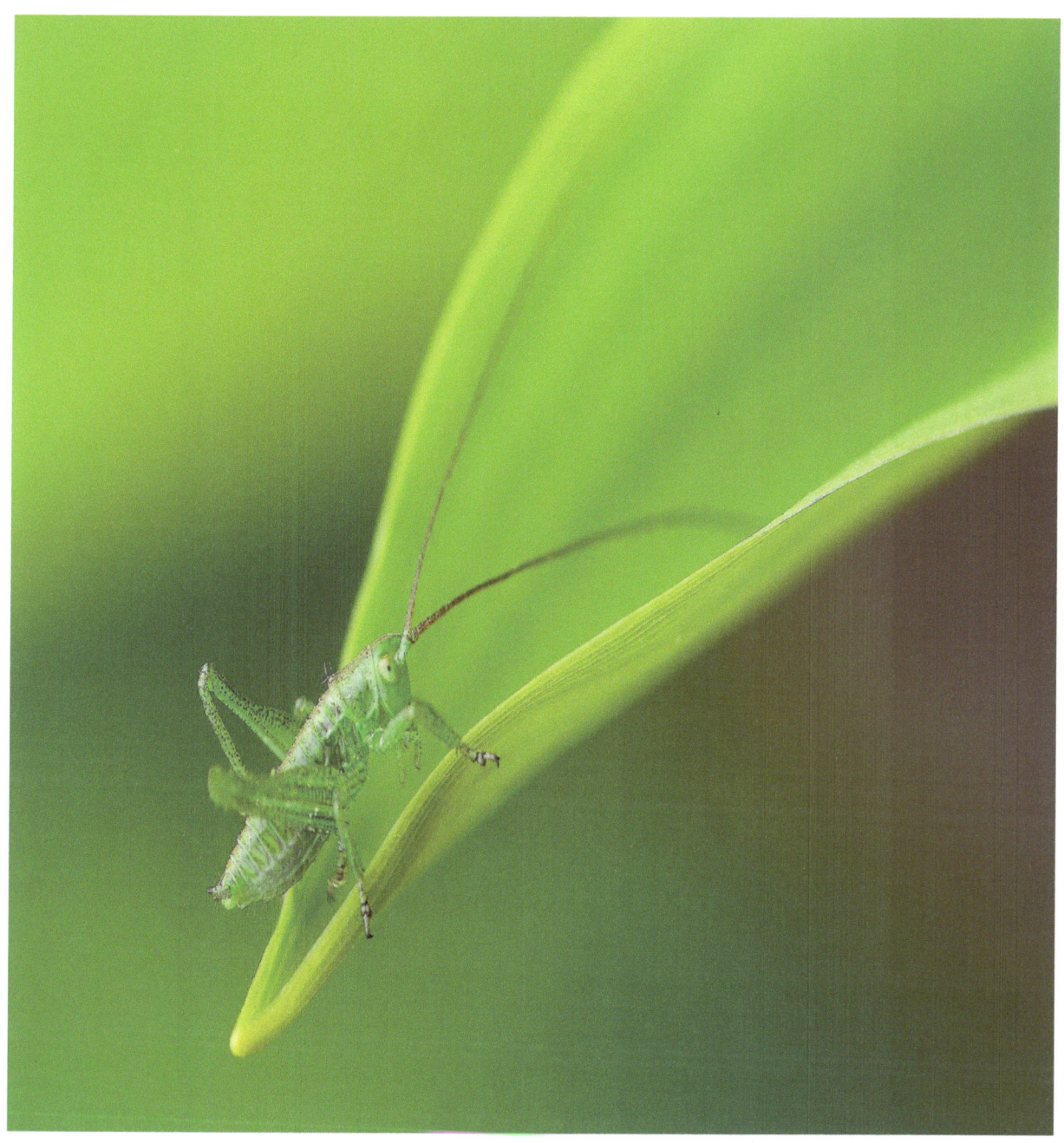

This grasshopper is the color green.

(15.)

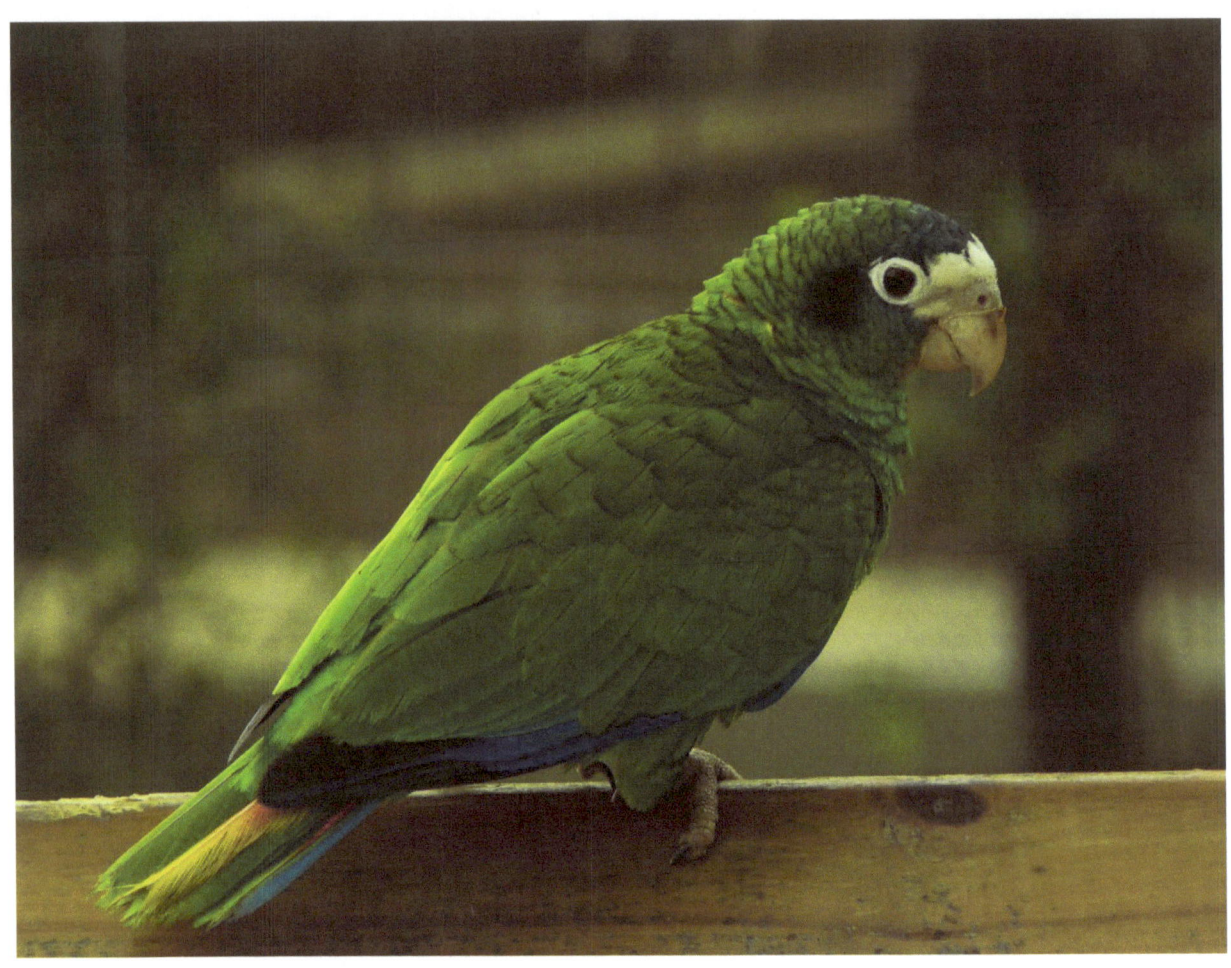

This bird is the color green.

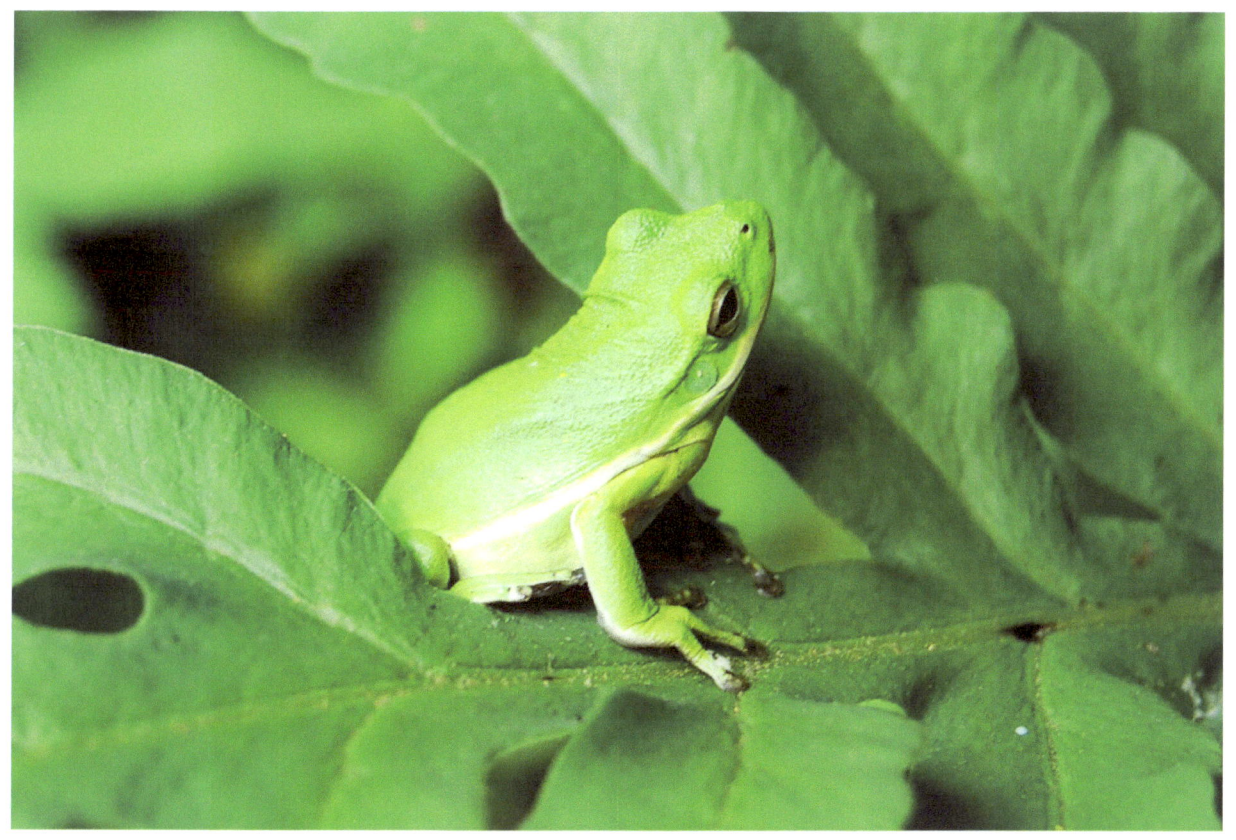

This frog is the color green.

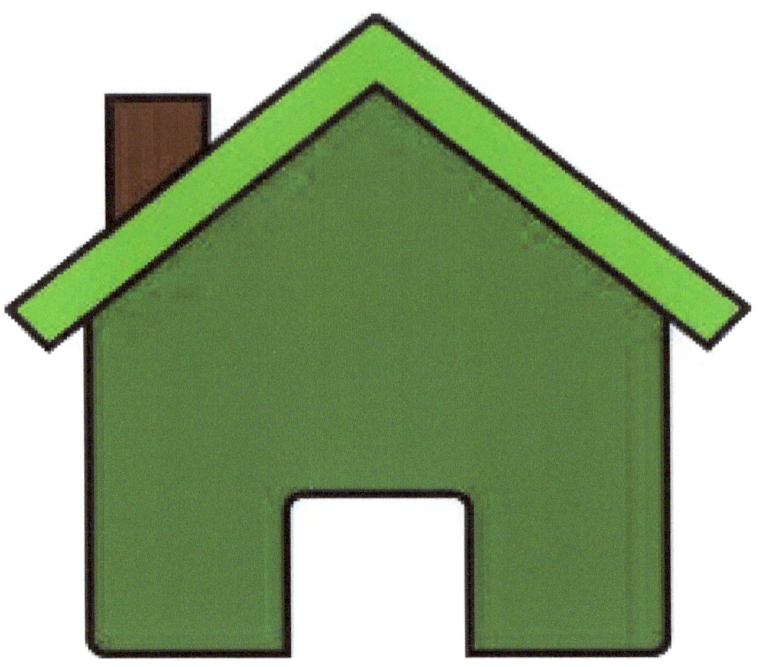

This house is the color green.

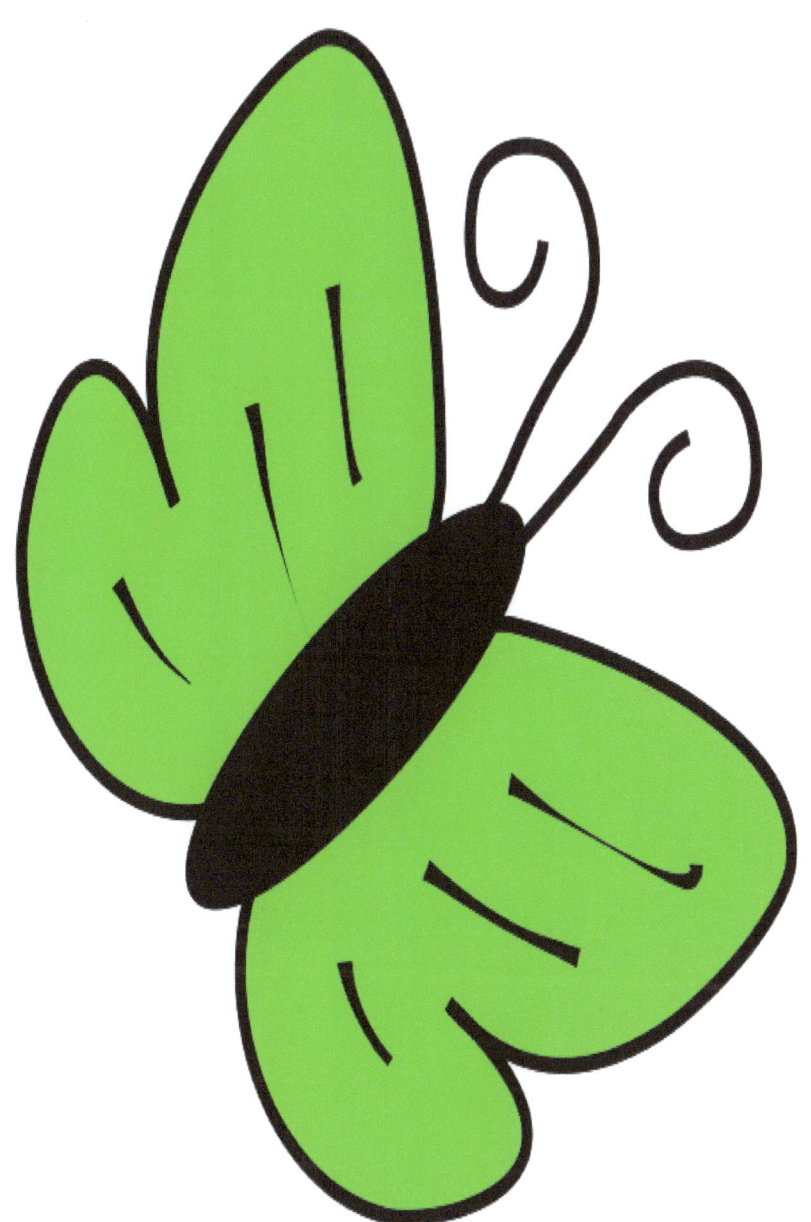

This butterfly is the color green.

This leaf is the color green.

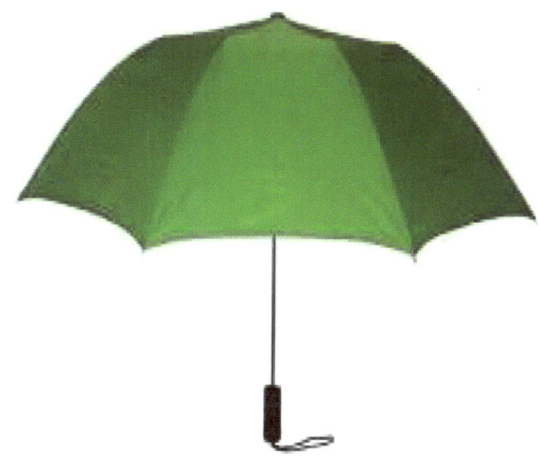

This umbrella is the color green.

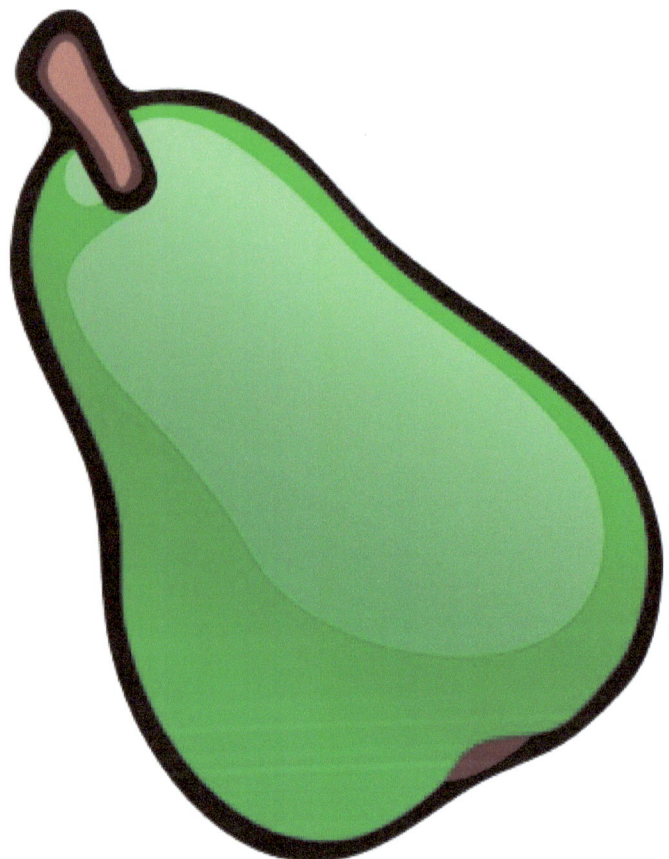

This pear is the color green.

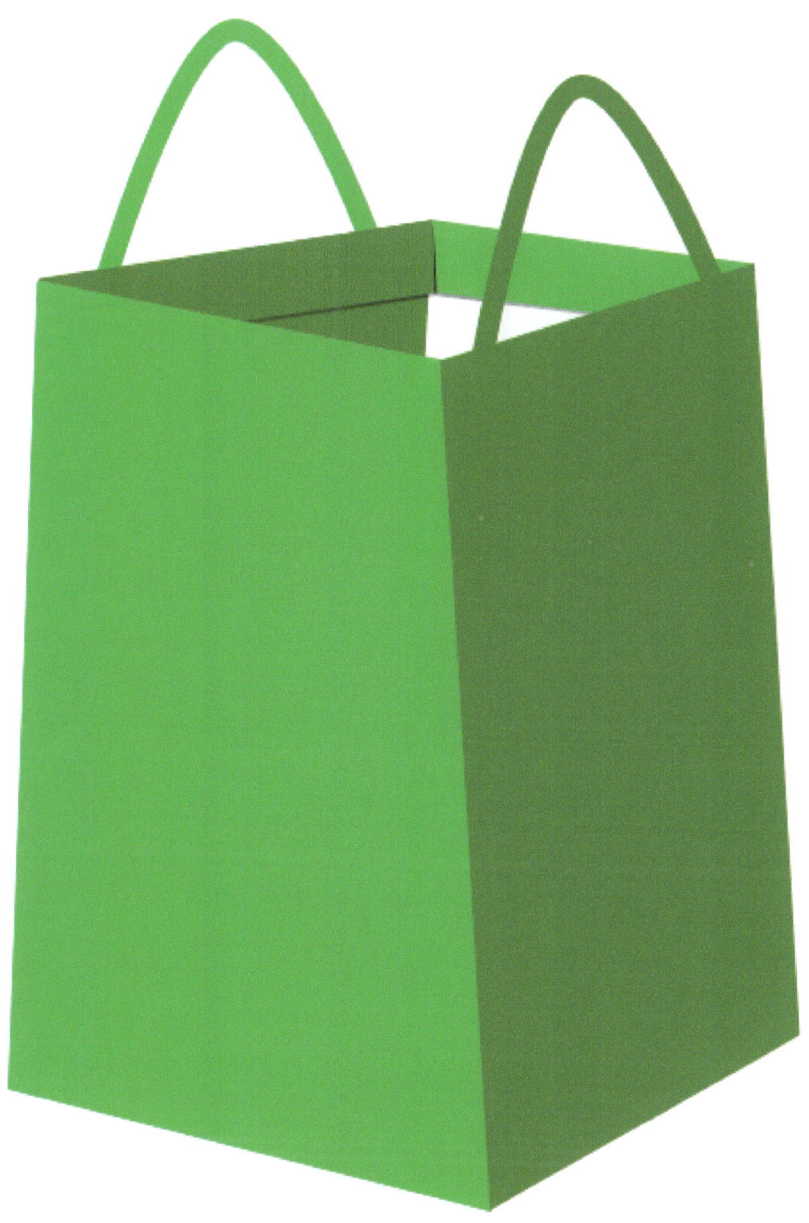

This bag is the color green.

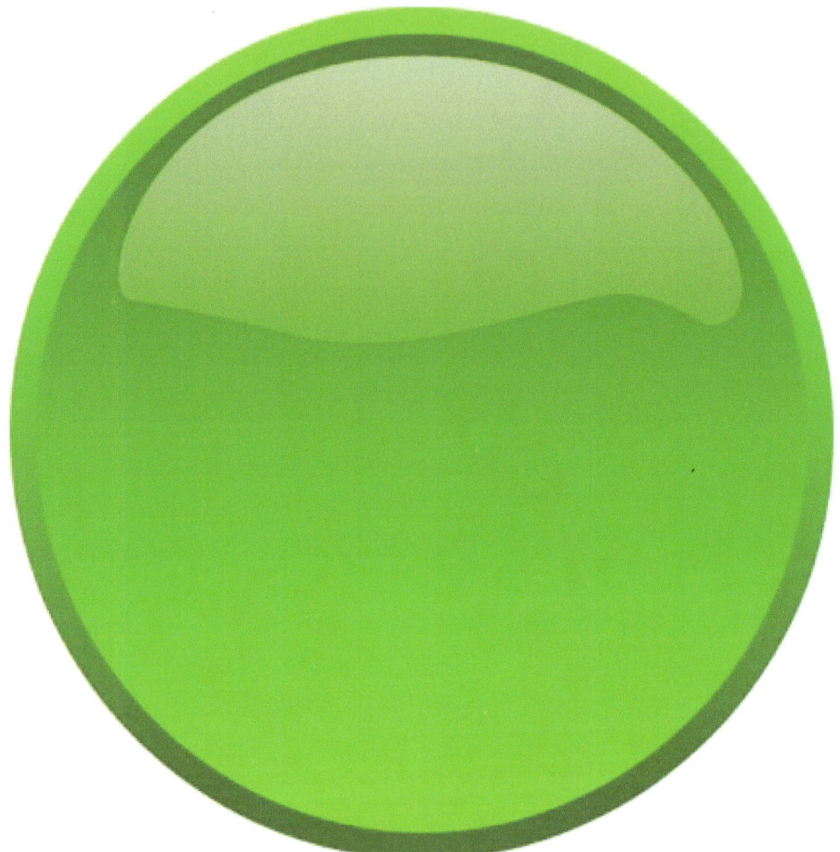

This button is the color green.

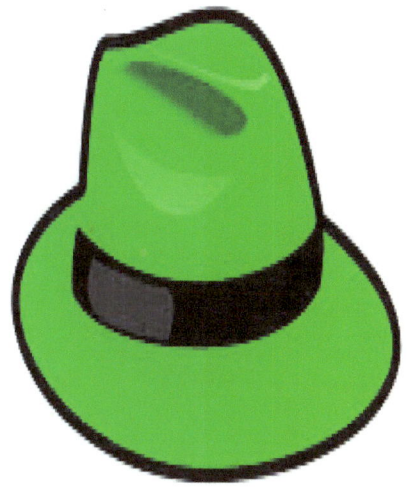

This hat is the color green.

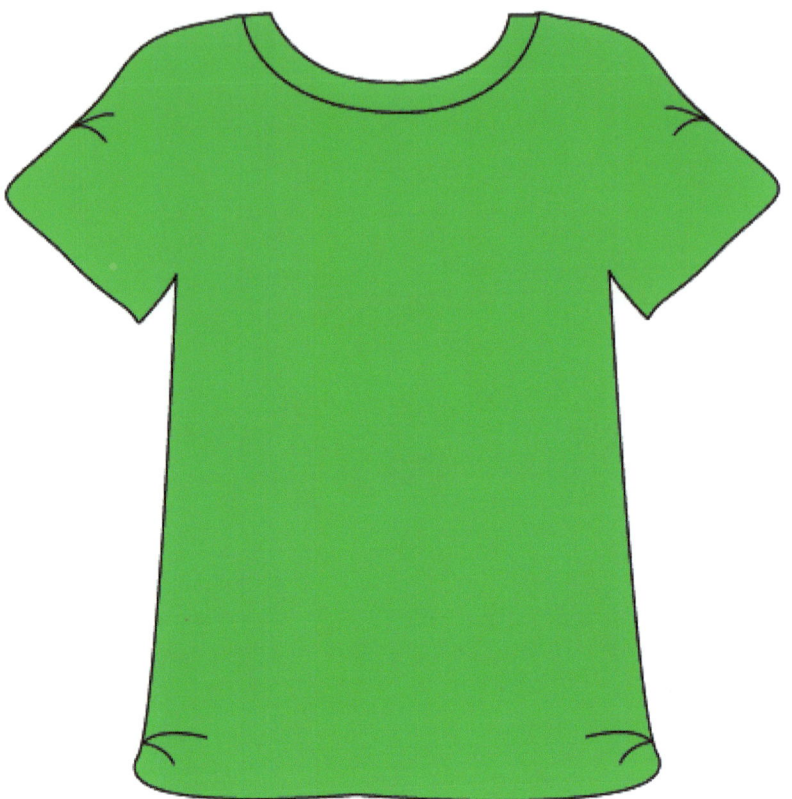

This shirt is the color green.

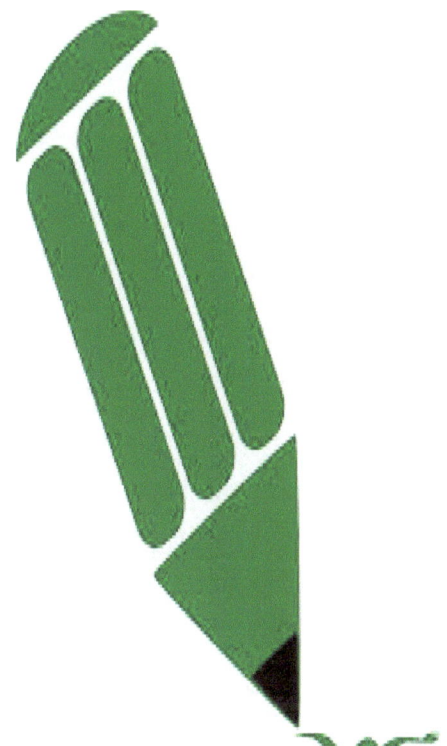

This pencil is the color green.

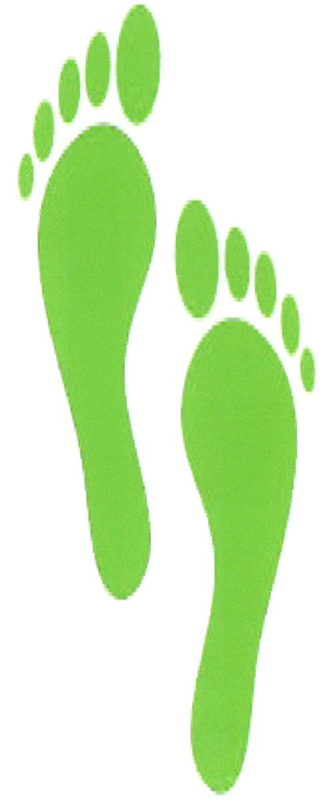

These footprints are the color green.

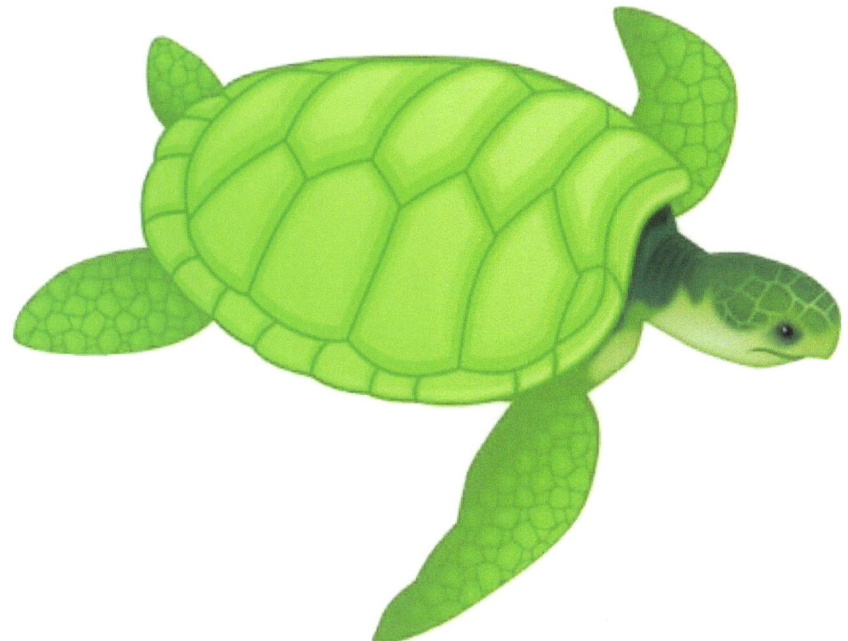

This turtle is the color green.

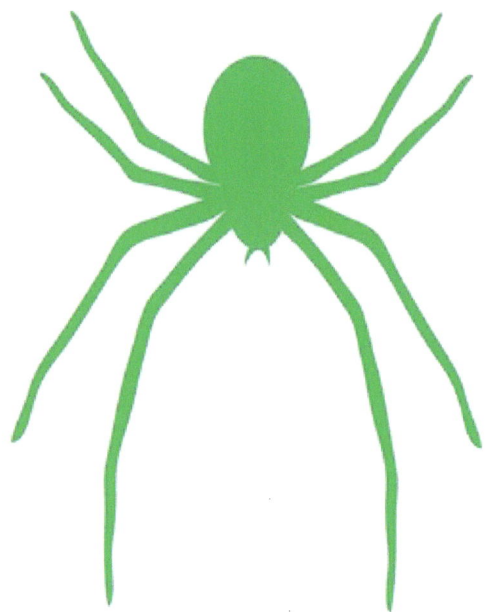

This spider is the color green.

(30.)

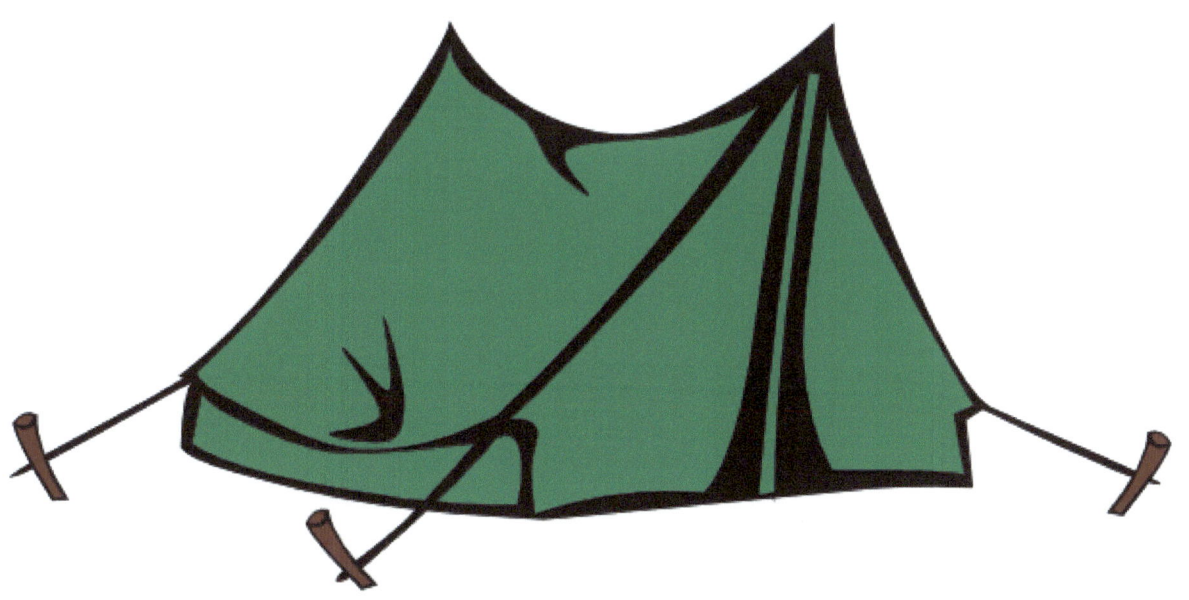

This tent is the color green.

(31.)

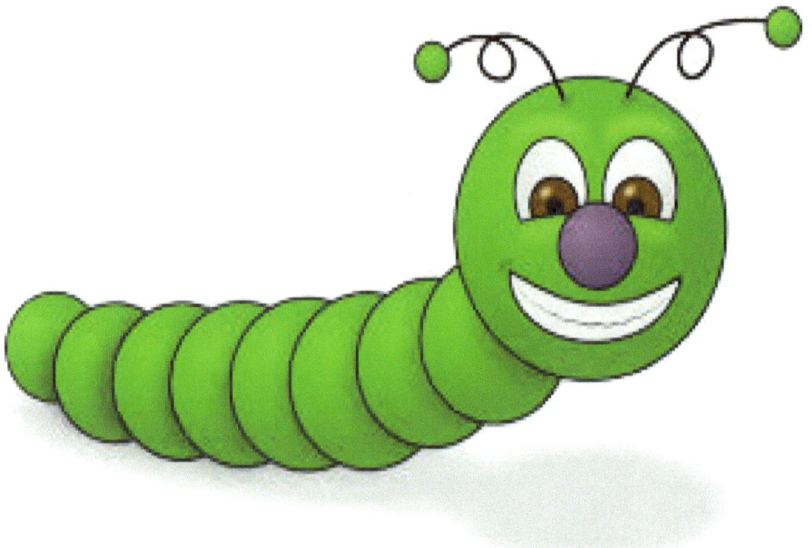

This worm is the color green.

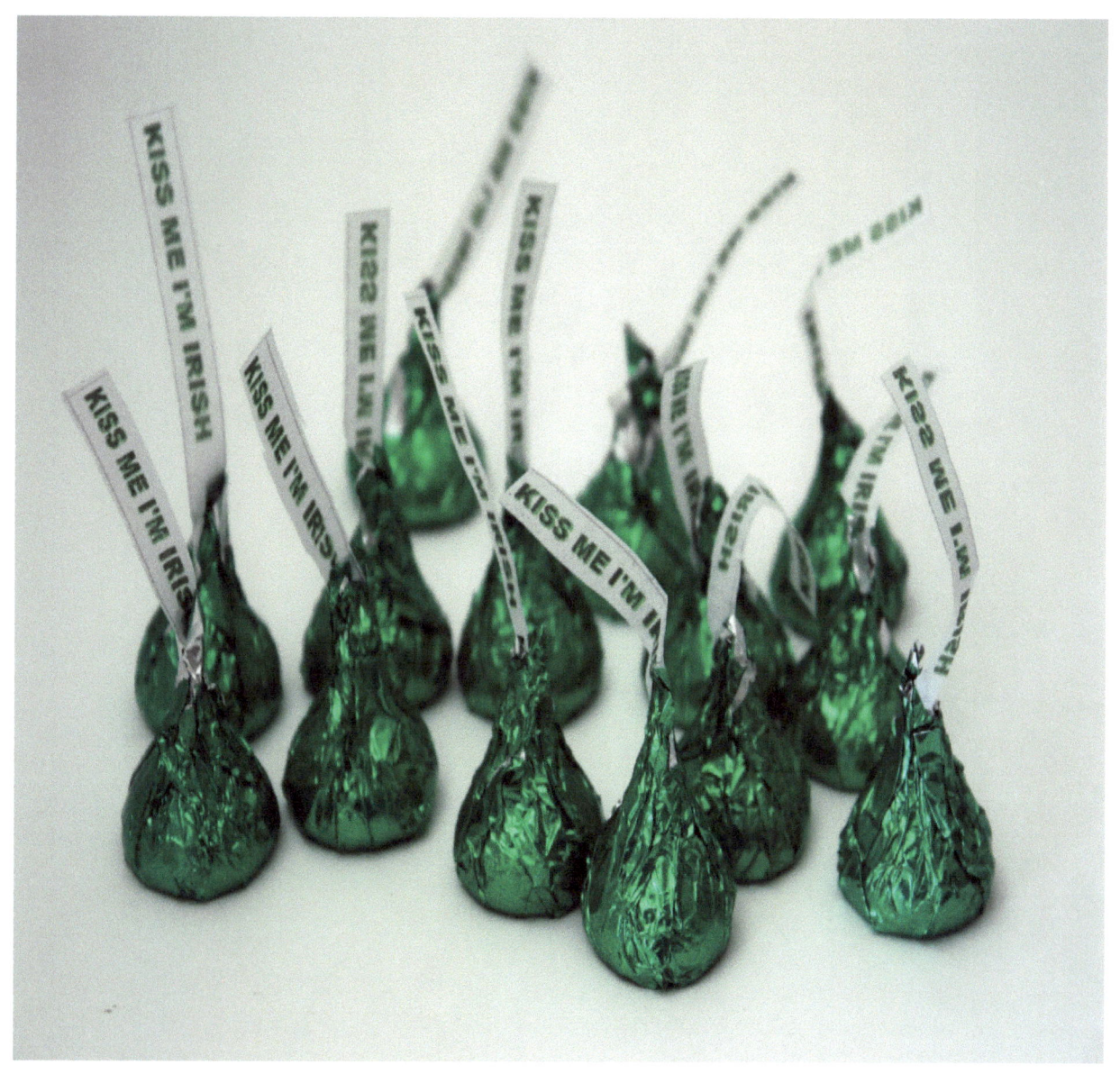

This is green Hershey's kisses.

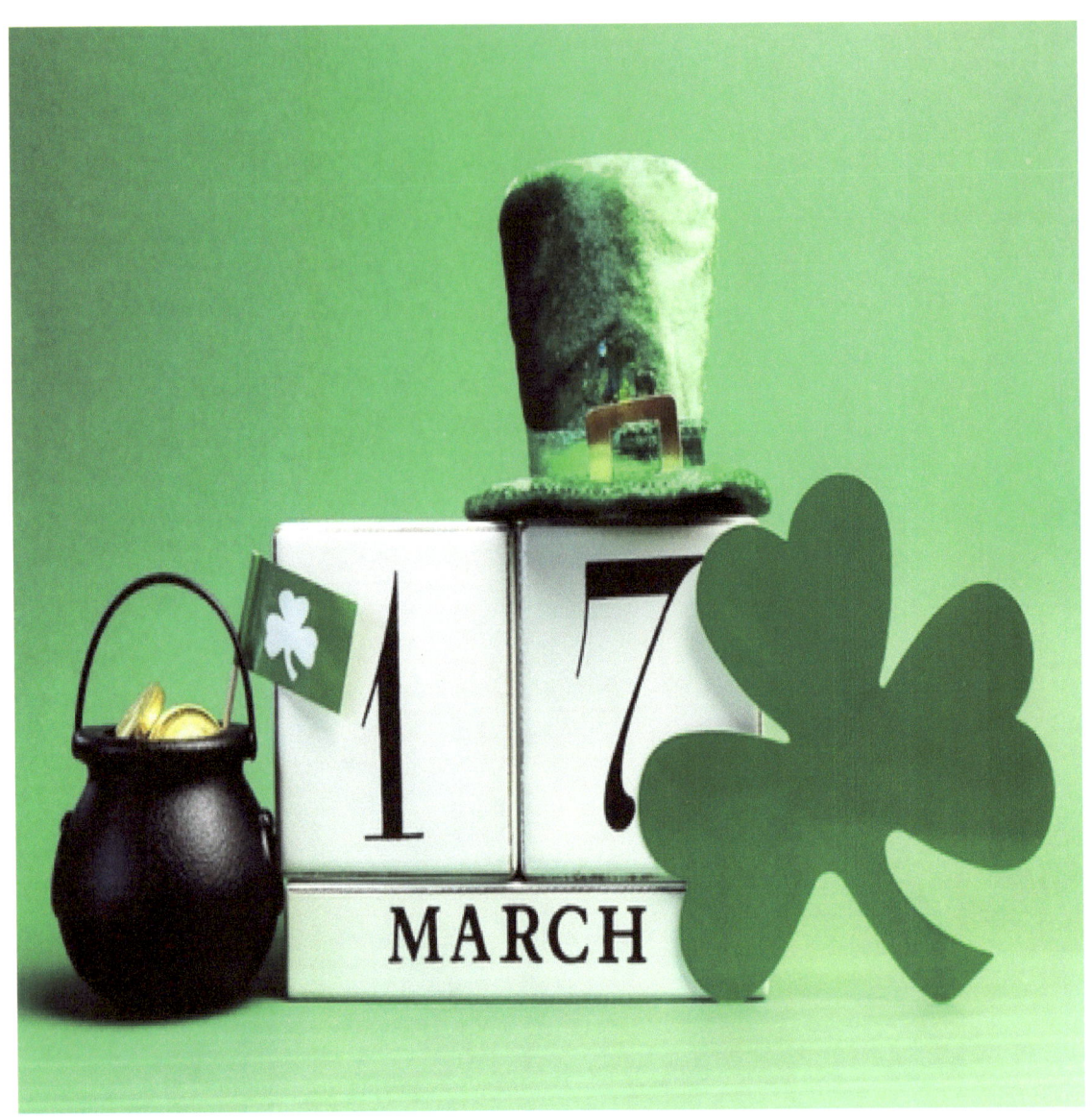

March is the month we're supposed to wear green.

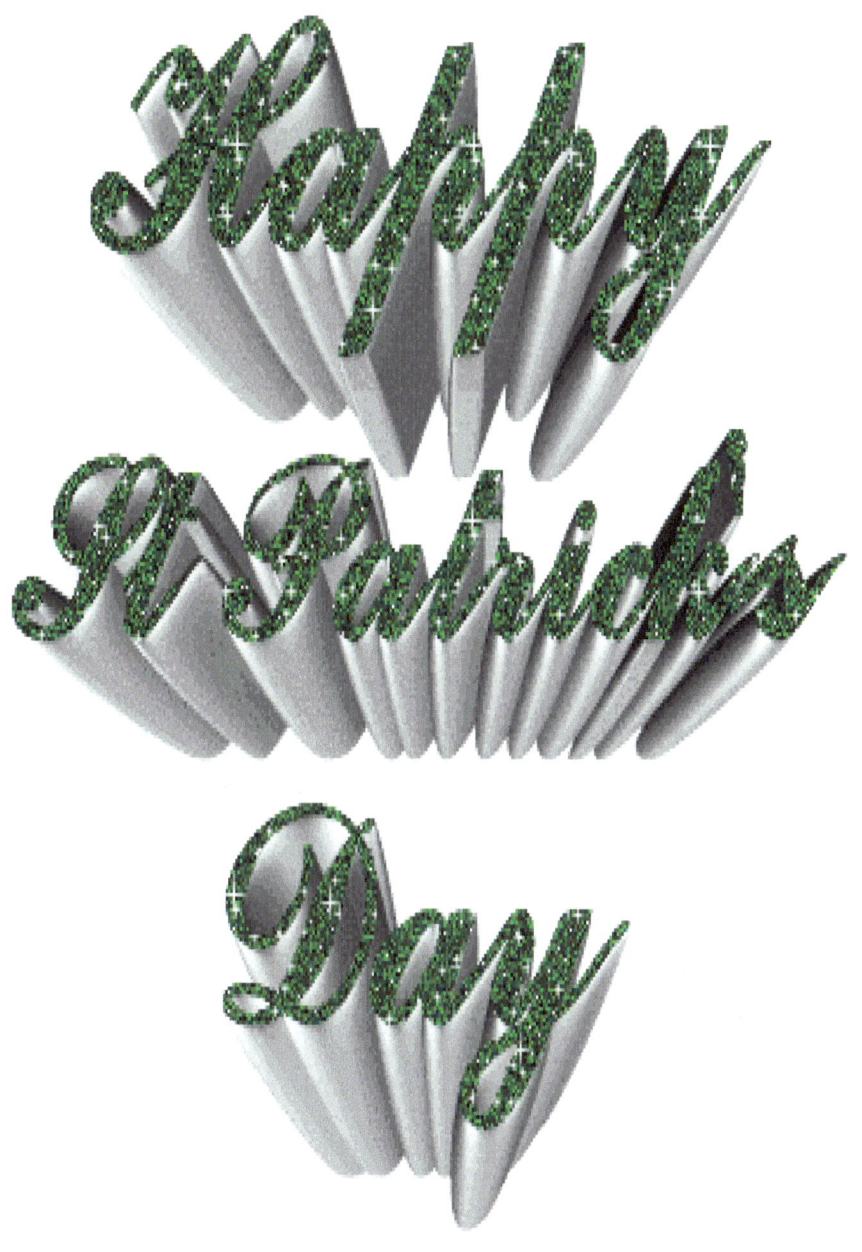

This is the color Green Happy St. Patrick Day.

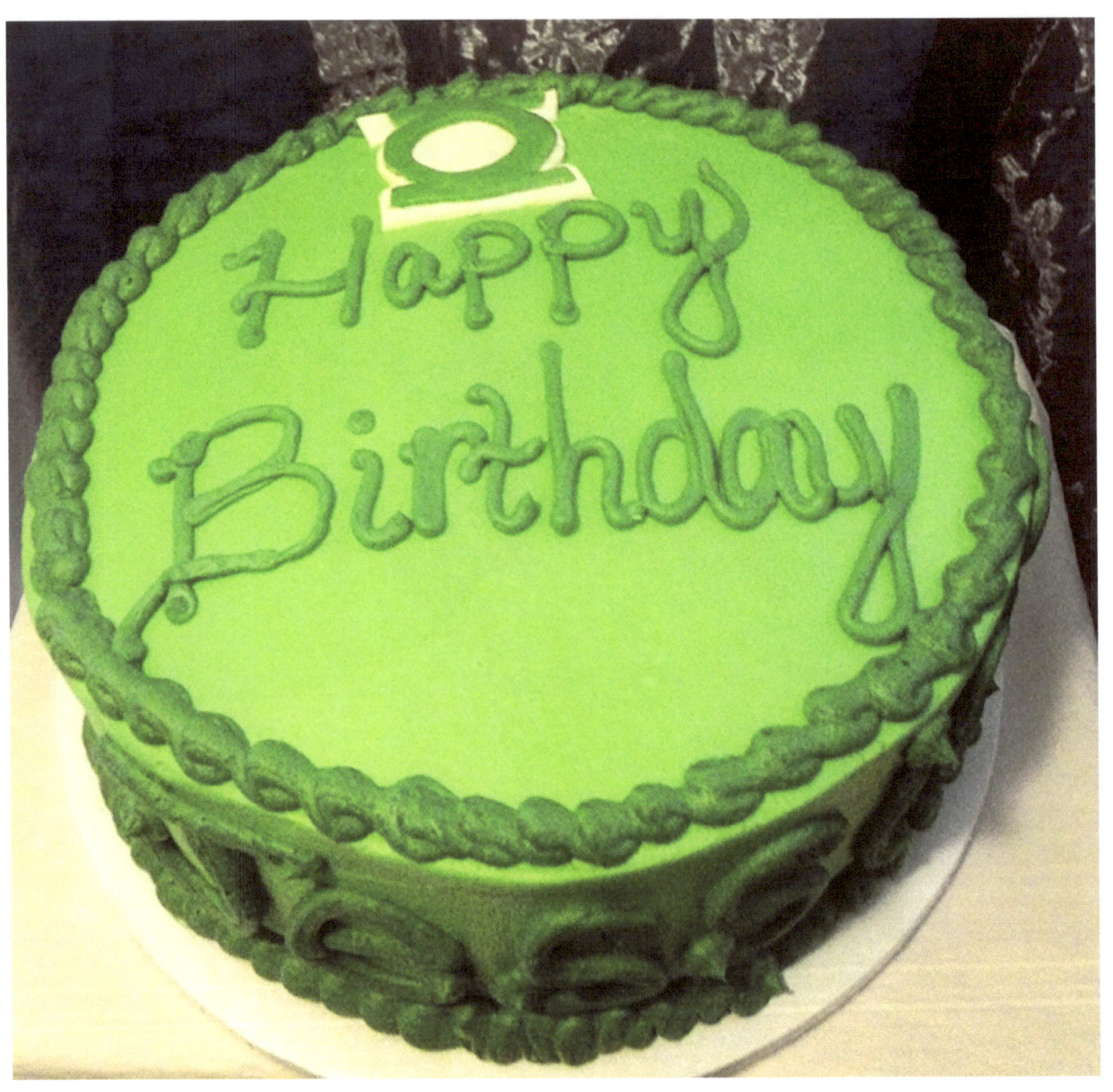

This is a green birthday cake. Happy birthday to all the peoples born in March.